OTT LUNCH

Written by Damian Harvey

Illustrated by Amanda Montgomery-Higham

Harcourt
Supplemental Publishers

Rigby • Steck~Vaughn

www.steck-vaughn.com

Once there was a giant called Otto.
Every day, Otto packed his lunch.
Then he went to work.

The other people packed their lunch, too.
Then they went to work.

Otto was very big and very strong.
He worked hard, and everyone liked him.
But there was one thing they did not like.

Every day at lunch, Otto ran off.
He ate lunch by himself.

The people asked, "Why does Otto run
off at lunch?
Why won't he eat lunch with us?
What is in Otto's lunch?"

The people said, "Next time Otto runs off, let's follow him."
The next day, Otto ran off at lunch.
The people went, too.

Otto opened his lunch.
He began to eat his food.
No one could see Otto's food.
But they could hear him.

"It's time to eat your hat!" Otto said.

The people saw Otto take a big bite.

CRUNCH!

Everyone could hear Otto crunching.

"It's time to eat your shoes!" Otto said.

He took an even bigger bite.

CRUNCH!

"Otto eats people!" a man called out.
"We must stop him!"
"It's time to eat you!" Otto said.
    He was about to take a very big bite.

"Stop!" the people called.

"You must not eat people!"

Otto turned red.

The people looked at Otto's food.

Otto was eating a gingerbread man!

"It's bigger than my gingerbread man,"
 a man said.
"Do you eat gingerbread men?" Otto asked.
"Oh, yes!" everyone said.

"Otto, why do you run off at lunch?"
asked a man.

"Why won't you eat lunch with us?"

"I am a big, strong giant," Otto said.
"But I eat gingerbread men."
"Everyone can eat gingerbread men,"
 the people said.
"Even big, strong giants can eat them!"

After that, Otto ate lunch with the other
people—well, most of the time!